CARING FOR THE ELDERLY

Practical Tips For Seniors and Care Givers

Joe Brown

© 2020

i

Caring for the Elderly

Description

The idea of caring for the elderly or aged parents does not evoke excitement for many people. They would rather be caregivers to infants and little children than the elderly. Although most normal people would want their parents to age gracefully into their 90s and beyond, a lot of people are ill-prepared to handle the challenges that come with taking care of seniors.

This book will expose you to proven methods and hands-on techniques that can help you build the right mindset and approach the task of caregiving as a benevolent and honorable one. Old people are humans and, like young people, they deserve to be treated with respect and dignity even as they grow frail and become dependent on others. This book provides you with the right tools – tips and mindset – and equips you to show kindness and give appropriate care to your aged parents and other seniors. As you diligently apply what you learn, your aged parents (or any elderly persons) will be happy that they spent their last years on earth under your warm care.

Contents

Introduction

As long as a person remain alive, old age is inevitable! It doesn't matter whether it is in good or bad health; a person who lives well beyond their golden age is likely to eventually rely on others for support. And it is not just moral support; in many cases, the elderly depend on others for almost all their needs.

In recent years, life expectancy has witnessed an overall improvement due to access to better nutrition and healthy lifestyles. So, more and more people are likely to grow into their 80s and beyond before they eventually die. While that is certainly good news, the not-so-pleasant aspect of it is that the responsibility of caring for these seniors eventually rests on adult children who are not well-prepared for the task.

Many people are somewhat aware that they will have to become caregivers to their parents at some point in life. But they never really make out time to prepare for that eventuality. This lack of preparedness is evident in the way many adult children try to joggle their roles. They spread themselves thin between caring for their children and spouses, handling their jobs, managing their social life, running personal errands, and tending to their aged parents. Trying to do all these tends to take a toll on them after a while and living becomes a humdrum of tedious activities.

Life doesn't have to be that way, as you will find in this book. You can enjoy being a caregiver while enjoying every other aspect of your life at the same time. Get ready to learn the ropes and apply the tips that can ease the task of caring for the elderly.

But beyond making your task as a caregiver easier, using the helpful tips shared in this book can also improve the quality of life of the elderly. It doesn't matter whether they are frail and ill or not; given the right type of care, it is possible for a senior to experience longevity, improved health, and significant independence. It all begins with planning well for the task of giving care.

If you are already feeling overwhelmed by the unexpected increase in your schedules caused by caring for an elderly person, it is easy to fall into the trap of resentment and caring for them grudgingly. It will be no surprise if you meet with some form of resistance from the person you are caring for. To avoid this, it is important to understand the mind shift necessary to maintain a sense of dignity for your dependent and how to draw the line to help you set healthy boundaries. You shouldn't have to ignore your needs while tending to other people's needs whether they are your kids, parents, or your elderly clients.

I invite you to view this book as part of your investment in learning the important skill set required to help the elderly to live out their last years blissfully regardless of their physical conditions. Caring for the elderly is an honorable thing to do – it should give you a sense of fulfillment if you do it rightly.

Chapter 1: A Shift in Mindset and Role

For many people, caring for elderly parents at home is usually the first option because it removes the cost of facility-based care. Secondly, many seniors typically prefer remaining in the comfort of their well-accustomed homes than being bundled off to a nursing home.

While it may be desirous to be surrounded by family members, caring for the elderly is not the most convenient thing to do, especially as the task of caring for seniors usually falls on adult children. These adults equally have their hands already full and might not cope well with the extra task of caring for older persons. But if your elderly relatives or parents must live in their homes or with their families for the rest of their lives, it means the task of caring for them must be borne by at least one person in the family. In many cases, this task falls on women than men. More women are involved in caring for both their young children and frail elderly parents.

As rewarding as the task of caring for the elderly is, it can be a very emotionally challenging experience. Without proper planning, most caregivers (especially women) will find that they are suddenly living for someone else and abandoning their own lives. Many women – mothers in particular – are already living their lives mostly for their young children and spouses. Add to that the responsibility of caring for an elderly parent, and it could be proverbial last straw that breaks the camel's back. In many cases, it doesn't take too long before the caregiver starts to experience resentment, irritability, hopelessness, anger, or some other form of emotional problems. This is particularly true if the nature of caregiving requires constant support. To significantly reduce the emotional complexities, a shift in the mindset of the caregiver is necessary.

A Shift in Mindset

Emergencies cannot be completely ruled out when dealing with the elderly. In fact, you should expect emergencies if you have an elderly person in your family. Proper planning can equip you for any eventuality and save you the need to run helter-skelter during emergencies. Typically, a "formal invitation" from your aged parents to be a caregiver is not usually the norm. Instead, an unexpected diagnosis or sudden bathroom fall might be all it takes to plunge you into the role of a caregiver. So, if you have elderly persons in your family, it is best to have it in mind that such cases can come up at any time.

Secondly, you must see the task of caring for the elderly as part of the normal cycle of life – the caregiver becoming the dependant. It is the natural order of things. You were once a baby who completely depended on your parents for the most simple and basic things. With time, you became dependent, and sooner you had kids of your own who depended on you. But the circle is not complete. Your parents (if they are still alive) will eventually become your "kids", so to speak. They will depend on you for the same things you looked up to them for once upon a time. And even then, the circle is still incomplete because, with time, you will also become a "child" to your kids.

Of course, it can be argued that you can simply hire professional caregivers to take care of aging parents. But even then, you are saddled with certain aspects of caring for them, for example, handling their finances, helping to decide which assisted living facility to engage, and so on. Normal people with healthy family ties cannot be completely divorced from caring for their frail and aging parents.

Switching Roles

If you have aging parents, your role is about to change (if it hasn't already). They cared and nurtured you when you were young. It is now time for you to care for them. But how exactly would you know when you need to give more care to your elderly relatives? Here are three ways:

1. Are you over 50? If yes, there's a big chance that your parents are anywhere around 70 and above. If this is true, you should start playing the role of a caregiver to them even if they are hale and hearty.

2. Even if you are not up to 50 and your parents are not too old, you need to switch roles as soon as your parents start having trouble with simple daily activities (for example, using the bathroom, bathing, running errands, preparing their meals, and so on).

3. If your dad or mum suffers any mental or serious physical health problems, especially those associated with aging, you will need to take on the role of a caregiver.

The best way to be sure that you are there for your aged parents or relatives when they need you is by checking on them regularly to see how they are faring (physically, mentally, and emotionally). You do not necessarily have to visit them to do this. Calling and talking with them will help you determine whether or not they require your help. By talking with them, you can figure out if they'll need constant support or occasional help. You will be able to also decide if you are in the right position to care for them or whether you will need to enlist the services of in-home care providers or other assisted living facilities.

Equally, you can observe them while spending time with them. By physically observing them, you can tell if they will need your support for their day-to-day activities. Remember that you once enjoyed unconditional love and care from your parents. If you are in the position to support them as they age, make it a point for them to enjoy your supportive role.

First Things First: Take Care of Yourself

You cannot give what you do not have – there's just no magic to it. Have you ever wondered why passengers in an airplane are always advised to put on their oxygen mask before attempting to help others with theirs? It is because you cannot successfully render any meaningful help to another person if you are unsafe or unfit.

Part of the mindset shift that makes your task as a caregiver less stressful is giving up the idea that caring for the elderly means sacrificing yourself –

your time, freedom, fun, and anything you enjoy. That notion constricts you and gradually sniffs life out of you! You don't have to buy into that idea.

Shift your attention from the doom and gloom that many people associate with giving care to the elderly. Yes, it can be emotionally and physically exhausting trying to get a grown man or woman to do the most simple or basic of tasks, but you are not meant to stick by their side at all times. You do not have to deny yourself the pleasures of life and the things you enjoy doing because you want to give proper care to an elderly person.

If there is one thing you must reinforce in your life when taking on the role of a caregiver, it is this: stay connected to your social circle. Burnouts can quickly occur once you put yourself in a position that makes you feel isolated. If that happens, your actions of caregiving will stem more from a place of obligation instead of genuine love and concern. But here is the complicated thing about being in that spot: you will end up beating yourself up for feeling that way. *"I am a terrible person for feeling less love for my parent who was there for me all their life."* Regardless of how many times you punish yourself for feeling that way, your isolated position puts you in a place where all you can think of is the fun you are missing out on.

You can avoid this vicious circle by setting yourself free from the self-imposed curfew that says you must give up your social life if you must care for the elderly. Take out time to go to parties (if you like parties), go for long walks, or have your idea of fun away from your dependent older adult. You are not a bad person for looking out for yourself! Don't allow your mind to trick you or anyone else to guilt-trip you into thinking otherwise.

But besides hanging out at social gatherings with family and friends, consider seeking out local support groups for caregivers. If you can't find one in your locality, join a support group online. There's a certain level of reassurance self-compassion that comes from knowing that you are not alone and others are equally sharing in similar experiences that you are going through. Support groups are a great way to minimize burnout.

Other practical ways that you can care for yourself and ensure that you have the right mindset as a caregiver include:

1. **Practicing self-compassion**: Caring for the elderly is very tasking; don't let anyone – not even your mind – tell you differently. Instead, notice your efforts and praise yourself or give yourself credit for all the complex, tough, and challenging work of caregiving that you do. Indeed, there may be times when you don't put in a 100 percent into the task of caregiving, but bashing yourself or allowing your harsh inner critic to run you down won't help either. Always keep in mind that you are human and you can't always be at your best all of the time. The most effective use of your time when you are not at your best is not engaging in self-criticism. Instead, it is taking out time to pay attention to your needs. You are not being selfish when you practice self-compassion. What you are doing is putting yourself in the right frame of mind that allows you to be more focused and balanced to properly discharge your duties as a caregiver.

2. **Practicing relaxation techniques**: It is possible for caregivers to experience a heightened sense of stress. It is not surprising to become overwhelmed by a mix of emotions as you attend to an older adult, especially if they are someone who once cared, supported, and provided for you. Seeing someone who was once physically and mentally strong and supportive now depending on you for their basic human need can stir up deep emotions in different people. Relaxation techniques can help to reduce the level of stress that can come from such experiences. Some of these relaxation techniques include mindfulness meditation, tai chi, yoga, or simply listen to guided audio meditations.

3. **Practicing breath awareness**: Breath awareness is similar to the relaxation techniques above. It is particularly useful when you feel stressed, irritable, or simply exhausted. Sometimes, the failing condition of your aged parent or relative might get you overly worried and affect your overall mood. Worry or anxiety does not help you or your loved one. Instead, it is a state of mind that can make you act irrationally or even alarm your loved one. To get you balanced and focused, practice being aware of your breath. Here's an example of how to do this exercise:

- Find a quiet spot where you will not be disturbed for about 10 minutes.

- Sit comfortably and let your eyes gently close as soon as you wish.

- Notice how your breath goes in and out effortlessly. It is normal and okay for several thoughts to float into your mind. Gently let the thoughts go and bring your attention back to how your breath moves in and out of you.

- Now, inhale slowly through your nose while counting up to five. Hold your breath and count up to five before exhaling while counting up to five again. If you feel any form of pain as you pause or hold your breath, skip the pause and simply breathe in and out for five counts.

- Repeat the process for about 10 minutes.

- Gently open your eyes and feel your mind and body rejuvenated as you return to your activities.

4. **Prioritizing sleep and nutrition**: When your activities begin to steal your time so much that you no longer eat and sleep when necessary, you are giving room for burnout. As much as possible, ensure that you get adequate sleep. To help improve your sleep patterns, practice any of the relaxation techniques discussed above just before you go to bed. You can also do a breath awareness exercise to improve sleep quality. Eating the right types of food and at the right time is also of utmost importance. You should not put your energy into caring for someone else while you neglect your nutrition. It is best if you can limit or completely avoid the consumption of refined sugars and processed foods. Unhealthy foods and junk foods increase

inflammation which in turn may lead to chronic stress and disruption of sleep.

Tips for Protecting Your Sanity

From the previous section, it would appear that caregivers are always saintly. But in reality, caring for the elderly can drive you nuts at times. While it is ill-advised to show disapproval, anger, or frustration in the presence of a senior, it is a good idea to let out your frustration through appropriate channels. To end this chapter, here is a small list of ideas that can come in handy when it feels that you are losing your mind (trust me; it will feel that way sometimes).

- Get a pillow. You will need something soft to punch once in a while. Do this in private of course!

- A trusted friend that can share hearty laughter with you and also give you their ears during your darkest moments.

- Watch hilarious movies to distract you from any worries, anxiety, or fears that may result from your task of caregiving. Make sure you avoid movies with difficult or sad parents or any movie that is related to caregiving. Your goal is to distract yourself especially when things become too hectic, not to remind yourself of your current situation.

- Create an "alone-time" and just be by yourself for an entire hour, if possible.

When you are done with your "alone-time" engage yourself in something that brings you joy such as dancing, gardening, painting and so on.

- Recall great memories or look at mementos that remind you of pleasant times. Spend a couple of minutes several times daily to do this. It has a way of reducing any stress you may feel.

Now that we are done with caring for the caregiver, let us now turn our attention to the actual task of caregiving.

Chapter 2: A Safe Living Environment

Making Changes in the Home

Frequent domestic accidents are some of the first typical signs that an older adult in the family might require extra attention. It is not uncommon for seniors to want to spend their last years with their families at home, rather than constituting nuisances or being a burden on their adult children.

Making changes for a senior can be difficult sometimes. It is not uncommon to meet with resistance and even end up getting angry or frustrated, especially when it is a big decision such as staying put in their home or moving in with you. It is a good idea if you can hire an expert care manager that can help to mediate differences over caregiving and adjustment options. On the surface, it might look like an easy thing to simply tell your parents to move in with you or make some major adjustments to their favorite room in their home. But when you are emotionally neck-deep in a situation, it is difficult to be objective and respectful at the same time without feeling like you are losing your mind!

But whether an elderly parent wants to spend the rest of his or her life in their own home or move in with you or a sibling, there is a need to make the living space safe for them. Usually, seniors living with a relative or family member do not require skilled support or professional care. Nevertheless, in addition to enjoying the companionship of a family member, the following living adjustments are necessary.

- Install anti-scalding devices in faucets and showers. Anti-scalding devices are good for protecting older skins from burns. In the absence of an anti-scalding device, you can set the temperature of water heaters to "low."

- Consider installing railings or grab bars near the toilet, in the shower or bathrooms, and hallways as well as other living areas of the home.

- Make sure to install lights that are bright enough to provide adequate lighting in the entire home.

- Install special smoke detectors in the home. Seniors are particularly very sensitive to carbon monoxide even in low concentrations. Unlike conventional detectors that are mostly set at frequencies that many elderly people find difficult to hear, modern smoke detectors are set to quickly wake up the elderly.

- Ensure that floors and surfaces that are easily exposed to water – bathroom floors, kitchen floors, and showers – are non-slip surfaces. Equally, make sure that stair surfaces are non-slip.

- Install stair climbers or ramps to aid movement in steep areas of the home.

- Consider installing elevated toilet seats and shower seats.

- Reduce the number of furniture in the home. Ensure that there is ample space for free movement in the house.

- Remove cables and loose wires from the floors. These can easily become booby traps.

- If you are a tech savvy-person, you might want to consider installing modern motion sensor devices that can be strategically placed in the home. Motion sensors do not have microphones or cameras. So, technically, you are not spying on or violating your parent's privacy. The device simply keep tabs on seniors to help you alley any doubts. With modern motion sensors, you can tell if your aged parent has been in the bathroom longer than usual, for example. Or if he or she hasn't stepped out of bed for a long time. Updates are sent to your mobile device to keep you abreast of happenings in your parent's home at regular intervals.

Suggested Living Arrangements

Living with a family member (or live-in support) is not the only option when it comes to making safe living arrangements for seniors. Other suitable options that can ease the task of caregiving on family members include:

- **Aging at home**: many seniors tend to opt for spending their last years in their own homes. If this is the wish of your elderly parent or relative, it is best to respect it. However, this choice may require making a series of adjustments to their homes to ensure their safety since they are mostly going to be living by themselves. Whether they have challenges with functional mobility or not, they will require support from professional caregivers or at least a family member.

- **Nursing homes**: this is particularly suited for seniors with some form of chronic health issues. Older people who need to live in an environment equipped with adequate medical support and care without necessarily living in a hospital can explore this option. Nursing homes are typically equipped with professional caregivers or nursing staff who are available around the clock. Nursing homes eliminate the time delays that can occur between emergencies at home and the arrival of medical attention. Such delays can be fatal.

- **Assisted living communities**: this option works well for elderly persons who are independent to some extent but still require some level of caregiving and assistance with their daily activities. The services of assisted living communities include offering group meals to seniors living together, rental apartments, housekeeping and laundry services, gym, and social activities. This community also helps seniors with transportation, bathing, dressing, and medication.

- **Independent living communities**: this option is best suited to independent seniors who are still active. It is a community of elderly people who buy or rent apartments or homes. Although these communities don't offer medical support (obviously because it is a community of fit seniors), they provide social amenities including clubhouse, gyms, social activities, and group meals. There is also the provision of transportation, laundry, housekeeping, yard maintenance, and security services.

Although, aging among family members is a great choice, sometimes, it might become necessary to look at these other options mentioned above, especially if providing care for the elderly will significantly disrupt your already established routines or if the elderly person in question requires specialized care.

Nevertheless, these options do not mean you care less for your parents or relatives. Instead, think of it as a win-win situation for all involved. This is also part of the mindset shift that is necessary for your own wellbeing. If you cannot accept the fact that sometimes, you need to be away from a loved one, then you might find it difficult to live your life without harsh self-criticisms.

Chapter 3: Helping With Daily Activities

To give proper care to an aging family member, you must consider their physical, mental, and emotional wellbeing. In this chapter, we shall focus on how to efficiently handle the day-to-day activities of the elderly to ensure that their daily living needs are appropriately met. These daily activities include:

1. Functional mobility – moving around as they perform daily activities such as sitting in and out of a chair, climbing into and out of bed, and so on.

2. Self-feeding.

3. Showering or bathing.

4. Dressing.

5. Personal hygiene – this includes grooming activities, styling or brushing of hair, tooth and mouth care, shaving, manicure and pedicure, and so on.

6. Toilet hygiene – this includes reaching the toilet on time, sitting and getting up from the toilet, self-cleaning, and cleaning up after themselves.

If a senior can perform all or some of their daily activities independently, then, by all means, let them do it. Do not deprive them of feeling useful at least to themselves. This is part of ensuring that their sense of dignity remains intact. Encourage them to do things by themselves as long as you are sure it is not injurious to their overall wellbeing.

However, in some cases, the person may have health issues that impair their mobility or become too frail to perform some or all of their daily tasks independently. That means you will have to provide the appropriate help they need to function effectively. This could mean giving care by yourself or enlisting the services of a trained caregiver.

The core of this book is focused on showing you the ropes of caregiving particularly for the elderly. Therefore, the following section will highlight some of the most effective methods of helping out with the daily activities of the aging person in such a way that eliminates unnecessary stress for you (the caregiver) and maintains the dignity of the elderly person. Striking and maintain this balance is necessary to ensure that you don't cross into a grudging caregiver who is simply doing robotic actions without a corresponding genuine feeling.

Whatever you do, keep in mind that each person might have a different situation from the examples in this section. Therefore, I strongly advise that you approach these suggestions as general guidelines. You might need to tweak one or two things to suit your situation and the older adult in question. The way to approach a relatively healthy aging adult is completely different from how you would care for a senior that is most incapacitated or who suffers poor health.

Giving Physical Help

It is often necessary to offer help physically, either by bathing, dressing, moving, or lifting the elderly person. At such times, it is important that you remember the following while lending a hand:

- Be slow, gentle, and deliberate when giving physical help. If you try to hurry up an elderly person, you are likely to create more delays.

- When necessary, give precise instructions and keep it brief as much as possible. For example, do not say, *"Turn around,"* when what you mean is, *"Turn and face me."*

- Always speak calmly and make him or her to know exactly what you want to do before you do it. For example, don't pull their clothes over their heads without first saying, *"Now, I'm going to remove your sweater over your head. It will cover your head briefly, but it will be quick you'll hardly notice."* You might unwittingly cause them to panic if you act too suddenly without first telling them what to expect.

- When you are trying to make physical contact with an elderly, try as much as possible to touch them from an angle where they can see you clearly – preferably from the front. Don't approach them from behind especially if they are not expecting you or if they are quick to forget things. Try and maintain eye contact with them for the most part of your interaction. That way, both of you can see and read each others' intentions and body language.

- If you have to lift an elderly person for any reason, be absolutely sure that you can do so on your own. If not, do not hesitate to seek help from others. You could ask a sibling, friend, or neighbor to assist you in moving or lifting the elderly person. If it is a case of emergency, it is best to call the paramedics or police.

- When you lift an elderly person, ensure that you engage your knees and leg muscles. Don't attempt to lift them by exerting your back muscles.

- Finally, don't forget to offer kind words of reassurance. Remember that the elder needs to know that they are aging gracefully and with dignity. Therefore, as they follow your instructions, let them know that they are doing great.

Preventing Loss of Items

As people age, it is common for them to start forgetting things including the location of items they use daily. It is a mental condition with many elderly people which is known as dementia and it can interfere with daily functioning. Some common symptoms of this condition include short-term memory loss, confusion, having a hard time finding the right words during conversations, apathy, difficulty with keeping up with storylines, difficulty remembering familiar landmarks or directions and being repetitive.

When you begin to notice these changes in a senior, be prepared to checkmate unintentional loss of stuff around the home.

Here are some ways you can do that:

- As much as you can, ensure that the house is kept tidy at all times. Even when things eventually get missing, they can be easily found in a less disorganized environment.

- Keep important items such as eye-glasses or house keys attached to a strap that can be hung around the neck.

- Make sure that you keep infrequently used closets and cabinets locked. Doing this will help to reduce the number of places where items can be unintentionally hidden.

- Make it a habit to check the pockets of their shirts and pants before dry-cleaning or washing. Valuable items may be forgotten in pockets.

- Ensure that you go through the contents of wastebaskets before disposing of them. It shouldn't come as a surprise to find missing items there.

- Get in the habit of keeping important items together or in the same place at all times. For example, always keep the TV remote on the side stool to reduce the frequent need to search for it. Or always keep house keys hanging close to doors so that seniors don't need to look for it when it is time to lock the doors.

- If possible, make two sets of important items available (for example, hearing aids, dentures, and eyeglasses), in case one gets missing and needs to be used urgently.

Suggested Technical Support

The advancement in technology can offer you great relief in the arduous task of caring for your aged parents and loved ones. You can leverage cutting-edge apps as well as fully functional websites that provide caregiving services, especially for seniors. This option is particularly useful if you have a very busy schedule as it lightens the workload on you as a caregiver. Although it is a more expensive option, your parents can live more independently with some of these technical supports. Note that mentioning these technical supports here does not mean that I endorse them. I strongly suggest that you do your findings or research before choosing any.

1. Telikin produces computers that require absolutely no tech knowledge to use. The computers have large touch-screen buttons and displays that are appropriately labeled with different functions. All a senior needs to do is touch a particular label, for example, EMAIL or VIDEO CHAT. The systems are pre-ready to keep you in touch with your loved ones even if they don't know how to use computers.

2. Lively is another tech company that makes tiny sensors that can be attached to many household items and locations in the home. These sensors provide updates through text messages or emails that keep you abreast of what is happening with your aged parents who are not living with you. They can be attached to the door of a refrigerator or kitchen cabinets to let you know whether your elderly parent has had any food or taken their medication. The tech company also offers a safety watch that comes with a one-touch emergency button.

3. StandWith is a mobile app that serves as a registry for caregiving tasks you will like to outsource. It is meant to coordinate help from other family members and friends who may like to offer you some form of assistance toward caring for the elderly. Without coordination, you may get too many offers for help in one aspect while other aspects suffer. For example, you may get another set of toiletries from a friend or family member when what you really need help with is someone to look after your dad or mom for a couple of hours. By listing the tasks that are available for outsourcing using the StandWith app, those who are available and willing to help with that such tasks will know exactly what form of assistance will be beneficial to you at that moment.

Chapter 4: Emotional Support

Encourage Engaging Activities

Regardless of your elderly parents' physical and mental health conditions, they are humans and shouldn't be caged or isolated. Don't ever treat them in ways to suggest that they are "eyesores" or unfit to mix with the rest of the world.

As much as you can, keep them connect to their social circle and actively engaged in their own lives. If they are strong enough to join some type of club, encourage them to do so. While it is a good thing to have independent seniors, it doesn't help much if independent living means retreating from participation in positively uplifting activities that were previously enjoyed. Encourage them to attend recreational, religious, or social events.

Give them the opportunity to engage others in mentally stimulating activities – let them discuss sports, fashion, and share their political views and ideas with other people. Do not shield them from healthy interactions.

Regular Visits

If your elderly parents live apart from you, make sure that you take out time to visit them often. Spending quality time with them usually has a more positive impact on the emotional wellbeing of the elderly than calling, writing, or sending gifts. Ensure that each of your visits put them in good spirits and uplift their moods. You can do that by sharing kind words with them (think about what to say before going for a visit). Share pleasant memories and also tell them how proud of them you are.

The positive thing about doing this is that it makes them look forward to spending quality time with you. That positive expectation is a powerful life-force that can give them a reason to live a bit longer. If your visits are not helpful or if there is nothing to look forward to, seniors may begin to withdraw from reality and that can negatively affect their emotional and physical wellbeing. Positive expectation calls forth energy and vitality – keep that in mind and do all you can to get your elderly parents in that frame of mind when you visit.

When you visit, take time to inspect the home for anything that can give you a clue to their overall mental and emotional wellbeing. For example, check to see if plants are watered and well nurtured. Try to see if there are many unopened mails or if the house is generally tidy or unkempt. Their physical environment is usually a reflection of their baseline emotional states.

As an added measure, you could build a good rapport with a few neighbors who could keep an eye on your parents when you are not around. But whatever you do, do not give your parents the notion that you are hiring someone to spy on them. Always check with them before introducing third parties into the mix.

Another way you can provide emotional support to the elderly is by doing fun things with them. When you visit or even during video chats, think of ways to introduce some type of fun activity. Take a lot of pictures with them, play around in their old clothes, dress funny, or do something goofy – just about anything that can make them enjoy the moment! Doing this doesn't only provide them with emotional support; it also eases the stress of being a caregiver. Hearty laughter shared could bring relief to both you and them and also take their attention away from whatever suffering or pain they may be going through. Creating fun moments add sunshine and color to their lives.

Chapter 5: Dealing with Resistance

The popular idiom that says, "You can lead a horse to water, but you can't make it drink," is true in every respect. As earlier mentioned, the task of caring for the elderly is quite challenging. Now, add to that an unwilling parent or loved one who doesn't want to accept care or help. How can you deal with a loved one who is elderly yet refuses help? Some people are naturally self-directed and would not want to be seen as weaklings that depend on others for support. To get the cooperation of such a person would require an understanding of the possible causes of the resistance to care.

Resistance to Care: Causes

Besides the innate desire to be self-reliant, several other factors may be responsible for resistance to care. These factors include:

- Loss of a spouse – refusing to come to terms with the loss of a spouse can cause resistance to care. This could be a case of beating up one's self or living in regret for the loss of a spouse.

- Loss of independence – resistance can stem from the fact that an elderly person feels they will become a burden to their families if they accept to be cared for. Giving up their privacy and adjusting to new sets of routines might be too overwhelming for them to deal with.

- The fear of additional cost – closely related to being seen as a burden to the family is the fear of additional cost involved in giving care. This fear might lead to feeling guilty about bringing an extra cost to the family.

- Loss of memory – dementia or other memory-related problems can cause resistance. The elderly person may find it difficult to understand why they need your care and help.

- Being stubborn – this is generally related to an unwillingness to let go of ego. Some seniors erroneously view accepting caregiving as a sign of weakness.

So, how can you convince an unwilling aging parent to be open to receive care? Here are some useful tips that you should consider:

1. Bring up the topic when you and your aging parent feel relaxed. A relaxed mind makes it easier for both of you to listen to each other and see the other person's perspective.

2. Assess what type of help is needed and what type of service will be most suitable. If your elderly parent is reluctant to accept care from facility-based care service providers, try to see if his or her needs can be met by hiring someone to live with them. You could also consider enlisting the help of a family member who can conveniently joggle caregiving with their current schedules.

3. Discuss the preferences of your aging parent. Remember that you are trying to get "a horse to drink water" – an act that can only be done willingly. Therefore, their

preferences must be taken into account. Your goal is to find a balance – a bridge, so to speak – between what you are offering and what they are willing to accept. Come to a compromise and make them understand that the arrangement is for their greater good. Most times, you will have to painstakingly explain using rudimentary examples and instances, especially if they are having difficulty remembering details.

4. Ask other family members, friends, and associates to help you convince them. You wouldn't want to be seen as someone who doesn't care about the wellbeing of his or her parent. Therefore, you should explore all avenues to get your parents to step down from their high horses. Don't throw in the towel if your aging dad or mom is not willing to discuss the issue with you. Bring it up at another time. If they are still not open to the discussion, talk to their friends and trusted advisers. With the right approach, someone will get through to them and make them see reasons to accept some level of care even if they are will still do many of their activities independently.

Effectively Managing Resistance

One of the ways you could manage your unwilling parent's resistance to care is by suggesting a trial run instead of starting with a full-blown caregiving service. You could ask him or her to hold off their final decision about refusing or accepting care until the end of the trial run. The goal is to give them a firsthand experience of the benefits of having help and care. At intervals, make sure to ask for their feedback and then address whatever concerns they raise if they have any.

You could also explain your needs to a senior who would rather live with you instead of accepting assisted living (in their homes or nursing homes). Get them to understand that you need to lighten your burden a bit and professional caregivers are a good option for both of you.

Sometimes, resistance to care is due to concerns about costs. Do your findings to see if the cost of care for your loved one is covered by some sort of government funding (such as Medicaid). If that is so, explain that fact to them to help relieve their concerns.

The above strategies might work for elderly persons with sound minds. However, if they suffer from dementia, it might be difficult to get them to see your point. They are likely to continue to resist your offer and put themselves in harm's way. If that is the case, get a doctor or lawyer to speak with them about receiving care. They are likely to listen to professionals than family and friends.

Chapter 6: Physical Health

Unless you double as a trained medical practitioner, always remember that your task as a caregiver does not include providing medical care beyond administering basic first aid. In cases where the physical health of an elderly person is deteriorating, it is advisable to let them live in a nursing home or a facility that can provide expert medical care.

Even seniors who enjoy good health still require assistance with their health. You might need to constantly remind them to take supplements or vitamins, or even medicines for common ailments. But great care has to be taken when it comes to medicines. A mix up can occur and the wrong medicine or dose can be ingested due to forgetfulness, poor eyesight, or drowsiness. To avoid this costly mistake, take time to label medicines boldly. Also, place medicines in separately marked drawers, if possible, to minimize occurrences of a mix-up.

Encourage seniors to get involved with simple physical exercises that are not too strenuous. It could be going for daily walks or even joining a walking group. Besides the health benefits of regular exercise, getting outdoors occasionally can help seniors feel better about themselves.

Sometimes, when seniors come down with common ailments that are not life-threatening (such as headaches, back pain, cold, and the likes) it may not be convenient to get them swift medical attention. You can take advantage of the Doctor on Demand support available on computers, tablets, and smartphones. It is a medical support service that offers a short video consultation with licensed physicians for a small fee. They offer referrals or prescriptions for simple ailments. This option can save you the additional trouble of driving your elderly parent to a hospital and spend several hours waiting for a consultation.

Foods, Allergies, and Special Medical Needs

If you are going to enlist the help of an expert or another family member, it is important for everyone involved in the task of caregiving for the elderly to properly understand what types of foods or nutrition the senior in question requires. If they have any special medical needs, you need to work with medical experts on the best ways to manage their conditions at home. If someone else is assisting in giving care, they should also be fully briefed about any allergies and medical conditions.

Independent seniors may insist on eating a particular type of food even if it is unhealthy for them. You must be firm but gentle when turning down their request. Be quick to remind them that you are doing it for their ultimate good.

If your parents are living by themselves, remember that they do not have the same level of stamina they once had for shopping, preparing, and cooking their meals. To reduce the expenditure of energy and cut down stress, many seniors choose to skip meals or simply opt for easily accessed junk foods that are nutritionally empty. This type of eating habit can lead to malnutrition.

To avoid nutrient deficiency, ensure that their pantry is stocked with healthy groceries. If you are not available to make their meals, hire someone or get another relative to do that for them.

Incontinences

Perhaps, one of the most physically challenging aspects of caring for an elderly person is dealing with a senior who doesn't seem to have control over their urination or defecation. But, if a caregiver keeps in mind the cycle of life mentioned earlier, it will help to start thinking of the dependent as a "big baby." Remember that if you show any sign of disapproval, it might negatively impact the ego or dignity of the elderly person. They may become emotionally withdrawn from you or deliberately choose not to share their fears with you for fear of being too vulnerable.

One of your goals as a caregiver is to become a confidant to your dependant. If you give seniors a reason to feel less about themselves, it would also cause them to doubt the trust they have in you and be less open to you.

While incontinences are often related to the malfunctioning of certain body organs, it is not necessarily the case for every senior. It could be that the elderly individual has forgotten how to respond to the urge to urinate or defecate. It is also possible that they may have forgotten exactly where the toilet is or even can't remember how to use the toilet. Maybe they may be having trouble getting their clothes off fast enough.

In any case, you should try and find out from a doctor if the problem is linked to drug side-effects, infections, or any other medical causes. If they are medically okay, you can consider applying a few of the following suggestions:

- Remind them at specific intervals to use the bathroom or toilet. Even if they claim not to need to use the bathroom, gently nudge and lead them to it. Remember to give them some privacy by either leaving them alone in the toilet or looking away. Doing this will encourage them to use the toilet.

- It is possible that they may forget why they are in the bathroom or toilet once they get there. Calmly remind them of the reason they came to the bathroom in the first place. Also, remember not to rush them along. It might take them longer than usual to empty their bowels or bladder.

- Ensure that they are always dressed in easy-to-remove clothing. Instead of pants with too many buttons, consider one with an elastic band on the waist that can be easily pulled down when the need arises.

- Consider leaving the toilet door open with the lights on to make it easier for them to find it, especially at nights. You could also place a bold picture of a toilet on the door of the toilet.

- Remove any objects such as wastebaskets or buckets from the toilet or bathroom that might confuse them.

- Always raise the toilet seat to make it easy for them to use.

- Be on the lookout for indications that he or she wants to use the bathroom. For example, repeatedly glancing toward the bathroom, becoming uneasy or fidgety, and playing with the fly on their pants. Also, pay attention to any sounds they might make (such as saying pee-pee) that indicates that they need to use the toilet.

- Consider buying them adult diapers as a last resort.

- If you have done all you can to make sure they use the toilet, but they still experience incontinences, refrain from showing frustration or anger. Understand that they are just as babies who simply can't help it. Make up your mind that such accidents will happen from time to time and it is okay. But beyond accepting that it is okay, make sure that you reassure the senior that there is nothing too serious about the situation. It was only an accident and it is okay if it happens once in a while.

Chapter 7: Safeguarding Their Finances

One of the diciest subjects for many people (both young and old) is money. Everyone wants more of it regardless of their age. However, older people are more susceptible to being defrauded of their money. And because money is a sensitive topic for many people, mismanaging it, being cheated out of it or losing it (especially to scams) can easily impact their emotional health and overall wellbeing. Great care must be applied when helping out with the finances of the elderly because of the likely emotional attachment to money.

Asking Important Money Questions

To get a proper handle on the finances of your elderly parents, here are three very important questions that you need to start asking right now.

The first question is: *"Have you made your will?"* Now, this question might be a bit uncomfortable to ask for a couple of reasons. First, it might be misconstrued to mean you are interested in what you can get as an inheritance after their demise. Secondly, it might subtly imply that you are thinking that your elderly loved one will soon die. And thirdly, it might just be plain taboo in some cultures. In any case, death is an unavoidable end. If you do not take the time to handle the awkwardness and any seeming uncomfortableness now while they are still alive, it might lead to more difficulty in managing or protecting their finances when they are no more.

If they don't have a written will, ensure that they do so immediately. However, be sure to approach the subject maturely and responsibly. If they already have a will, make sure that it has been updated within the last five years. It is equally important to know exactly where or who is in custody of the will.

The second question is: "*Where exactly are all the monies?*" You can't safeguard or manage finances that you can't track. Begin by going over their most recent tax returns. This will give you a good insight into their assets and liabilities. Start making a list of all their accounts – 401(k), checking account, savings account, credit cards, and so on. Ensure that you have the passwords or access to secure documents containing their passwords and other sensitive information, especially if they bank online. Also, collect the phone numbers of each bank's customer service line.

Lastly, ask: "*Who are your trusted advisors?*" It is better to get this information directly from your aging parent while they are still alive as that is the surest way to know who to reach out to for support and input when the time comes. Collect the names, contact details, and phone numbers of your parent's accountant, business partners, and trusted adviser, and even spiritual advisers (if they have one). While you are at it, you should also get the names of their lawyers, main doctor and other medical specialists, especially if your parent has several medical conditions.

Steps to Effectively Handle Their Finances

- No one likes to think that they are losing it even when they are growing older and gradually losing touch with reality. It is, therefore, important to broach the topic of helping with their finances with extra care. Approach the issue by making it clear that your goal is to protect rather than control their finances. Whatever you do, ensure that you talk things through with your elderly loved one before something unpleasant happens to their finances.

- Once your elderly loved one accepts your offer to assist them with their finances, follow up by making things official. Consider the following options:

  - Power of attorney: the document that gives you the legal backing to decide what happens to your elderly loved one's property and money. The power of attorney can be revoked by your loved one if they choose to do so.

  - Guardian of property: an order from a court appointing you as the guardian of your loved one's property after determining that your loved one is incapable of managing their properties and finances. This legal authority also makes you accountable to the court.

  - Living trust trustee: a revocable legal authority that empowers you to make decisions about assets in a trust. Your decisions are only limited to the assets listed in the trust.

  - Representative payee: an authority conferred on you to manage benefit checks from state or federal governments. This applies only if your elderly loved one receives such benefits from government agencies. This authority is limited only to managing the monies from the government and not any other assets belonging to your aging parent.

- After taking any of the legal routes to make things official, you assume the responsibility of your elderly loved one's finances and properties. It is expected that you must act in their best interest at all times without letting yourself to be motivated by a conflict of interest.

- Educate them about the different scams such as identity theft, annuity fraud, lottery scams, telemarketing scams, phishing scams, home repair scams, predatory lending scams, charitable donation scams, Medicare fraud, and other fraudulent investment schemes. Always respectfully remind them to consult with you before making any decision that involves investing huge capital. Ensure that you get periodical copies of their statement of account, especially their major bank accounts. If you notice any huge money withdrawals, you can hold a conversation with them about it.

- Finally, remember that it is their finances and properties. You are only there to represent their best interest. Therefore, learn to always respect their wishes. Don't force your wish on them. Always keep in mind that you are not in complete control – you are merely assisting. The best way to get your elderly loved one to trust your judgments and suggestions is to reassure them that you will always act in their best interest. Also, carefully explain to them their authority and rights – help them to understand that although you are representing them, they still have the legal authority to cancel or revoke your powers. Helping them understand this will build more trust in you.

Conclusion

You cannot prevent your parents from growing old (or even dying eventually) no matter how much you love them. But you can help them age with dignity, make them feel useful to themselves and others, and possibly extend their lifespan even if it is for a couple of months. Achieving this feat is not the easiest thing to do. A lot of physical and mental preparation goes into planning. Even at that, the actual execution – the process of giving care – can still be an overwhelming experience a lot of the time.

However, you can significantly reduce the likely stress associated with the entire process by applying the suggestions in this book. It doesn't matter if you are already actively involved in caregiving or you are expecting to take on the role any time soon. The tips shared in this book can be the difference between happily doing something rewarding and grudgingly doing tasks you would rather not perform.

I strongly suggest that you begin with the shift in mindset first before attempting to give care to anyone. And if for some reason, you are already caught up in the task of giving care with a mindset that is unhelpful to you and your dependant, it is never too late to set things right. A task is simple or difficult to the extent anyone thinks it is. It would be almost impossible for someone who thinks he or she is going to give up fun, enjoyment, and real living just to take care of an elderly person, to think of caregiving as an exciting or simple task.

With such a wrong notion, it is not surprising for that person to slip into a state of self-neglect. There is little to no zest for life. After all, their future remains bleak as long as they are stuck as caregivers to the elderly. Many caregivers – mostly mothers – who find themselves trapped in this thinking pattern tend to experience a downtrend in their emotional and physical health. Over time, they tend to suffer from weight gain due to improper nutrition, fatigue, social isolation, and might even develop sleep problems.

Caring for the elderly first begins with caring enough for yourself to not neglect your mental, emotional, physical, and overall wellbeing. It is only when you are balanced that you can give proper care to any other person. Get the right mindset and the rest of the tasks will naturally become easier.

Many elderly people do not really need much from you. A lot of them simply want to feel like they used to feel a few decades back. You can help them feel this way by simply giving them a listening ear and genuinely caring for them in the way that dignifies them.

The expenditure of time, energy, and love in the care of an elderly person is never a wasted effort. Regardless of what belief system you subscribe to, the undisputed fact remains that whatever energy you give returns to you in one way or the other. Elementary science teaches that energy is neither created nor destroyed – it only changes form. If you give love and care to another, especially one who has labored for you in time past, you are bound to receive love and care in ways that might even surprise you!

Finally, keep in mind that you do not have to bear the burden of caring for the elderly alone. Regardless of whether you have support from other family members or whether you are an only child, you can still get support from other sources – professionals, experts, and tons of information – as suggested in this book. These resources are available to help ease your task of giving care to the elderly. Seek out these caregiver supports and leverage them to help your elderly parents or relatives to age happily and gracefully.

References

1. Harvard Health Publishing, (2018). *Self-care for the caregiver*. Retrieved March 4, 2020, from https://www.health.harvard.edu/blog/self-care-for-the-caregiver-2018101715003

2. Aging In Place, (2020). *A guide to caring for elderly parents*. Retrieved March 5, 2020, from https://www.aginginplace.org/a-guide-to-caring-for-elderly-parents/

3. Huffpost, (2017). *Sanity-saving secrets for caring for your aging parents*. Retrieved March 5, 2020 from https://www.huffpost.com/entry/guide-to-caring-for-elderly-parents_n_6315930

4. Mayo Clinic, (2020). *Caring for the elderly: Dealing with resistance*. Retrieved March 5, 2020, from https://www.mayoclinic.org/healthy-lifestyle/caregivers/in-depth/caring-for-the-elderly/art-20048403